THIS

BOOK OF
SHADOWS

BELONGS TO

_____

_____

_____

WICCAPEDIA
JOURNAL

A BOOK OF SHADOWS

SHAWN ROBBINS

LEANNA GREENAWAY

STERLING ETHOS
New York

STERLING ETHOS
New York

An Imprint of Sterling Publishing Co., Inc.
1166 Avenue of the Americas
New York, NY 10036

ISBN 978-1-4549-3235-2

Distributed in Canada by Sterling Publishing Co., Inc.
c/o Canadian Manda Group, 664 Annette Street
Toronto, Ontario M6S 2C8, Canada
Distributed in the United Kingdom by GMC Distribution Services
Castle Place, 166 High Street, Lewes, East Sussex BN7 1XU, England
Distributed in Australia by NewSouth Books
University of New South Wales, Sydney, NSW 2052, Australia

For information about custom editions, special sales, and
premium and corporate purchases, please contact Sterling Special Sales
at 800-805-5489 or specialsales@sterlingpublishing.com.

Manufactured in China

2 4 6 8 10 9 7 5 3

sterlingpublishing.com

Picture Credits – see page 256
Interior design by Christine Heun
Cover design by Elizabeth Mihaltse Lindy

"An it harm none,
do what ye will."
—*The Wiccan Rede*

This Book of Shadows is your very own journal or diary for jotting down and recording your spells. When you cast a spell, write down all the details of the ritual, such as the date, the ingredients you used, and the phase of the moon. Leave a space underneath to record the results.

Before you start, following is a brief overview of the essential materials, tools, and tips to keep handy while preparing and casting your spells (these are covered more in-depth in our comprehensive book on Wicca, *Wiccapedia: A Modern Day White Witch's Guide*).

ESSENTIAL TOOLS

There are some implements witches simply cannot live without and quite a few more they may just like to have, although your spells and rituals will still work even if you use the bare basics. The required tools vary from spell to spell. There are a few rituals that don't require any implements at all, but for most, a selection of candles and herbs is generally kept close at hand, as well as tools such as the pentagram (to represent the five elements), crystals (to energize the area), and salt (to sanctify the space).

THE ALTAR

A base to work on, called an altar, is highly recommended. You should create your own altar and personalize it to your taste with whatever charms and objects speak to you.

Some witches born under a fire or earth sign prefer to cast their spells directly on natural wood, while others like covering their altars in cloth. If you do opt for a cloth, the best color to use is lavender or deep purple, thought to be the most positive color to attract spiritual fulfillment. It is also associated with chakra balancing and healing.

If an item's position on the altar is not specified in the following list, then just place it in a spot you feel comfortable with. Except for certain items, modern Wicca is quite flexible about the arrangement of tools on the altar.

THE PENTACLE

One of the most essential items a witch uses when casting spells is the symbol of a five-pointed star, known as a pentacle or pentagram. The five points of the star represent the five elements; spirit is the topmost point, and the other points, moving in a clockwise direction, are water, fire, earth, and air. Most witches tend to use the pentacle in the more familiar upright position that, if you look closely, resembles the form of a human: the top point of the star is the head, the outer points represent the arms, and the lower points correspond to the legs.

When casting spells, it is always best to have this symbol on your person or somewhere on your altar. You can either draw a simple pentagram or, if you are an artistic soul, create a more ornate centerpiece with painted glass or something similar. As you set up your altar, place the pentacle directly in the center so that you can arrange the other items all around it. The size of the star doesn't matter in the slightest.

Whatever kind of pentagram you choose to use, you should first "charge" it. This is a straightforward procedure that will cleanse and bless the pentagram and imbue it with magickal energy. The best way to do this is to leave your pentagram outside overnight in your garden or on your front porch or window ledge during a full moon phase. You can also charge other tools, such as crystals and talismans, this way to give them extra potency. Once the pentagram is charged and placed in the center of the altar, it will ward off negativity and act as your source of protection.

CANDLES

Candles represent the elements fire and air. Fire is a powerful element, so when a spell is recited over a lit candle, the message is transported to the universe much more forcefully and the desire directed back to us in due course. In Wiccan circles, this is called a candle ritual or candle magick. Most spells will include a candle or two, or even more, so always have a selection of different colors at hand. Traditionally, you start with one main white candle on the altar (usually centered toward the back) to neutralize the energies. There is no need to inscribe or anoint this candle, but blessing it with water is a good idea. To do this, dip your fingers in some bottled water and run them over the candle while saying, "This candle is now cleansed and blessed." Dry the candle with paper towels.

Each candle color has its own significance and therefore tends to work better for a particular problem.

GOLD, ORANGE, AND YELLOW: Healing, for both the mind and the body. Self-confidence and self-esteem. Fathers who may need a little help with parenting. Communication. Education. Finding lost property. Improving writing skills.

SILVER AND BLUE: Increasing psychic abilities. Issues that have to do with home and family. Women, pregnancy, and motherhood. Safe travels.

RED: Confidence and courage. Increasing sexual energy. Arousing passion. Protection against being attacked; protection against rapists and domestic violence.

PURPLE: Protection in general. House blessings. Invoking spirits. Business and work issues. New jobs.

PINK: Encouraging romance and attracting love. Creating harmony in relationships and marriage. Enhancing beauty to appear more physically attractive. Improving musical talents.

GREEN: Successfully managing wealth and money. Nature and garden spells. Passing driving tests. Success and achievements.

BROWN AND BLACK: Banishing evil. Stopping harassment or bullying. For a swift transition when moving house. Strengthening self-discipline, such as when dieting or stopping smoking.

WHITE: White candles can be used for anything at all, as white is a neutral color. You can replace any color candle with white if you don't know what color is the best for a specific spell or you

Preparing Your Candle

Before you cast any spell with a candle, it is important to prepare the candle first. To begin, cleanse it by wiping it with a clean damp cloth to wash away any unwanted energy. Take a sharp knife or pin and inscribe your desires onto the wax. Anointing the candle by dipping your finger into a tiny drop of oil (witches experienced in essential oils might use a special type such as lavender or citronella, but common vegetable oil works fine for beginners) and run it around the base of the candle. Now it is time for the words of your spell, otherwise known as the incantation.

Opening a Spell

A good way to begin a spell is by doing something we call casting a circle. Once you have all the items you need on your altar, take hold of either a quartz crystal or your wand in your right hand and stand quietly in front of your work space for a moment. Wave the crystal or wand over your objects, making the shape of a large circle in the air to enclose all of the magick inside the circle and keep out anything negative. There is no need to say anything at this point. If this is done in silence, it enhances the ritual without adding any confusing elements.

You can cast a circle either before or after you light the candle, but it is best to light the candle after you cast the circle so you don't risk setting your clothes on fire. Once your candle is prepared, you light it and speak the incantation you inscribed on it, repeating the words seven times. You can write anything you want on a candle, but beginning the incantation with "I desire" holds a magick all its own.

INCENSE

Burning incense while a spell is in progress is an absolute must. Its magickal properties help create the perfect atmosphere and boost any spell's potency. If you have trouble finding the right one for your spell, simply burn sage to cleanse your work space.

BASIL: An aromatic scent used for attracting wealth and prosperity and in fertility rituals.

EUCALYPTUS: Centers and balances emotions; excellent for helping make decisions.

FRANKINCENSE: A wonderful spiritual disinfectant. Can be used generally with

any health spells. If you are trying to ward off coughs and colds, burn it in a different room from where the patient is sitting to avoid irritation from the smoke.

OPIUM: Induces sleep and invigorates your psychic senses.

SAGE: Used as a smudging stick or burned as incense, cleanses your space in preparation for a spell. Its magick automatically dispels any negative energy.

SANDALWOOD: A warm, gentle, woody fragrance to relax you and ease distress.

YLANG-YLANG: A sweet and heady perfume that enhances any love spell. Use for attracting new love, harmonizing marriages, and healing impotency problems.

SOIL AND WATER

These substances symbolize the natural elements of earth and water and bring balance and harmony to your work space. A small bowl or an eggcup of garden soil should sit to one side of the pentagram, and the water—in a similar vessel or chalice—should sit on the other side.

SALT

Salt is a fantastic source of protection and is used in many spells to banish anything evil. Either sprinkle a little sea salt over your altar cloth or put some on the altar in a small bowl.

OPTIONAL TOOLS

CHALICE

Symbolizes fertility; in times past, its bowl represented the womb of the Goddess, the base signified our world as we know it, and the stem suggested human rapport with the spirits. Can be used to hold magickal water, but for casting spells to help someone get pregnant, fill it with fresh basil leaves instead.

CAULDRON

Probably the most recognizable symbol of witchcraft after the broomstick, today, the cauldron can be used as a vessel for making infusions and potions (although a microwave can also be used for many such spells). For spells that involve burning herbs, or to store herbs, the cauldron, typically fashioned from copper or cast iron, is still a useful object.

BELL

Used primarily in banishment spells, a bell can be rung to indicate that a spell is about to begin or tinkled repeatedly around the home to get rid of unwanted vibrations. It really can settle down a bad atmosphere and leave a place feeling calm again.

ATHAME

A ceremonial knife, typically black-handled with a double-edged blade. Some witches inscribe their candles with the athame or use it to cast a magickal circle around the altar before commencing a spell. To cast a magickal circle, hold the knife in your right hand and draw a circle clockwise over the altar, a few inches above the items on it. An athame works by conducting your power through it, and it is to be used only for magickal purposes—not for peeling potatoes!

WAND

A witch wouldn't be a witch without a wand. By tradition, wands are usually crafted from the wood of the willow, elder, apple, or cherry tree. Today you can easily buy a wand online or in a specialty store, but the real magick in a wand is channeled into it by its maker, so, if possible, try making your own. You can craft it from any tree branch that you feel an affinity for, and you should always thank the tree for sharing its wood with you.

Wands come in many shapes and sizes; the width is not that important, but the length of the wand should measure from your elbow to the tip of your index finger. You can carve designs into the wood or smooth it down with sandpaper before finally varnishing it and then charging it in the same way you would a pentagram. Make your wand as ornate or as rustic as you like.

For spell-casting purposes, the wand is used as a summoning tool and also to bless and charge objects. Before a ritual begins, you can touch each object on your altar with the end of your wand to transfer its natural earthly energy to the items and add a little extra magick. Some witches like to "draw down the moon" prior to casting a spell. This is a very old tradition that involves standing outside during a full moon phase and pointing the wand at the moon. It is thought that the moon's power charges the wand, making its magick more powerful. (See pages 24–26.)

BROOMSTICK

In witchy circles, the round-bottom broomstick, or besom, as it is more commonly known, is actually a fertility symbol, long used by female witches in fertility rites and to sweep away negativity. The brush corresponds to the female genitalia, and the staff is associated with the male phallus—therefore it is a symbol of the male and the female combined. Often a besom was propped up near the hearth to keep evil energy from entering through the chimney. Some modern witches still follow this practice, but many just display the besom as a Wiccan home decoration and embellish it with pretty flowers and dried herbs. Of course, besoms always were and still are popular at handfastings, where couples jump over the broom to display their union.

CRYSTALS AND GEMSTONES

Crystals possess a pure, natural magick. These are not just worn as jewelry, but often placed on our altars to support a spell. You can use any size crystal or stone; the results will be the same. Make sure to wash your crystals once a week or so. Crystals can absorb energies around them, so just as we need to wash to stay clean, you need to wash your crystals. You can put them in the bath with you (to be cleansed of external energies and infused with yours) or simply soak them in a bowl of water. When the crystals are not in use, be sure to respect them. Keep them in a special velvet-lined box or some other luxurious container.

Following are the nine most common stones that witches tend to use on a daily basis.

AMETHYST: This lavender-purple crystal has a gentle vibration and can be used for healing or to help calm stress and nerves. Amethyst can be placed near the stressed or ailing person or worn next to the skin. After the crystal has been worn for a week, rinse the stone in tepid water every evening for seven days and then let dry it overnight. When the healing process is done, leave the crystal overnight in the garden on a full or new moon to recharge it.

CITRINE: The "cuddle quartz," as it is often called, carries the energy and colors of the sun. It is a harmonizing stone that can make you feel at peace with the world. If you are lonely, hold a piece of citrine and feel the energy of love come into your soul. If you are angry with someone and want to vent your spleen, then citrine will calm you. This is the stone of abundance, good luck, and inspiration, so when witches want a bit more money energy, they use citrine along with money spells.

HEMATITE: This shiny black, slate-gray, or silvery-red mineral is used for safety during astral travel and to ground you once your spirit returns to your body. This crystal is very good for people with circulatory problems or anemia. It's also excellent for memory and mental stimulation, so witches wear hematite while performing spells that may be difficult or lengthy. If you were a witch in a previous life, by wearing hematite you may be able to tap into a previous existence and drum up some of the old spells and potions you used in the past.

LAPIS LAZULI: This rich blue stone has been treasured throughout history and is still held in high esteem by witches; we are very respectful of its powerful energy. It wards off negative vibrations and, if worn at bedtime, can bring vivid dreams of other lives and links to soul mates who may not have reincarnated at this time. Lapis alleviates migraines and problems with the throat, and it helps with ear infections too. But its main effect is to bring inner knowledge of other worlds. If you are seeking to enhance your psychic abilities, always wear this stone in jewelry form, and your insight will naturally develop.

MOLDAVITE: Although there is no absolute proof, this rare and precious natural glass gem, bottle-green in color, is thought to be extraterrestrial, formed from a meteorite impact. Because there is only a small, finite source of moldavite in Central Europe, it is sought after and rather expensive to purchase. You will have to be very grounded in order to wear this stone, because its power can easily overwhelm more sensitive individuals. You can use moldavite to enhance psychic ability or to connect with your guides in dreams.

MOONSTONE: Connected to the moon and its lunar phases, moonstone is a very mystical crystal. It has depth and translucency and is used to encourage premonitions during dreams. When you practice divination, you can wear moonstone earrings and rings to increase your psychic powers. This is a very feminine crystal, linked to the reproductive organs, the menstrual cycle, and female hormones. It can also be useful to help restore anyone who has gone into shock, or simply to calm volatile energies.

QUARTZ (CLEAR): Quartz, one of the most common minerals on earth, is considered an essential part of any witch's crystal collection. It is a multipurpose stone that can be included in almost any spell to bring about a positive result. Quartz is wonderful for balancing emotions, especially if you are trying to heal  painful feelings or if you have problems with self-esteem. This crystal amplifies magickal wishes and will bring extra power to any spell. Use it to tap into a higher consciousness and to keep in touch with your spiritual side.

ROSE QUARTZ: Pale pink and related to all things romantic, rose quartz sweetens one's mood and brings a calming influence to jittery brides and grooms. Witches use it to attract a beloved to themselves in spellcraft. When a witch is handfasted, she often carries a wand with a piece of this stone attached somewhere on the tip.

TURQUOISE: Turquoise is used mainly to ward off the evil eye or to protect yourself from negative people or influences. If you feel threatened in any way, use turquoise as an amulet. It can also purify the air and clear out heavy spiritual clutter. Turquoise is good to use if you have moved into a new home, to balance the energies and clear any negativity left behind by the previous inhabitants. It can also be carried as a protective measure when traveling.

FEATHERS

Because most of our spells invoke angelic energy, placing a selection of feathers on the altar will entice our angels to visit us. You can color-coordinate the feathers with the candles you are using in a particular ritual or simply use white for purity and peace. Here is a simple spell to summon your angel or guide:

Take a few white feathers and scatter them on your altar. Next, place five purple or lavender candles on the table or work surface and arrange them in a circle. Light the candles and visualize yourself surrounded by a purple light. Focus intently on your problem for at least five minutes. Now recite these words:

Angels of love and beauty,

I call upon you this day to help ease my burden.

With your inspiring power and influence,

show me the solutions I seek.

Then, in your own words (or in a poem you've devised, if you like), go on to describe the kind of help you want. Try to leave nothing out. Remember, the angels can only help us with our dilemmas if we ask them for their help. They are morally bound not to act on our behalf without our asking, because that would be taking away our free will.

Close the spell by saying:

So mote it be.

Let the flames burn for an hour (do not leave unattended) and then blow them out. Although this spell is simple, it is very dynamic if performed correctly, and within a few short days your problem will diminish and things will start to improve. If you want to make extra sure that the angels are listening, you can repeat this spell and relight the candles the next day.

HERB POUCHES AND WISH BOXES

Creating pouches and wish boxes is a lovely way of weaving magick to get your heart's desire. When you combine lots of objects and then cast a spell over them, you are merging their collective powers and bringing about a more intense ritual.

Boxes and pouches are traditionally filled with herbs or spices. Many herbs and spices have unique magickal properties and, when used in conjunction with a spell, can make the ritual more effective and potent. To make sure you always know the right substances to use, it's important to keep a list of them and what they influence in your Book of Shadows. You'll find a list of the most commonly used herbs and spices in magick below. Fresh herbs are best, but the dried varieties are acceptable if fresh is not available. When concoctions call for more than one element, you can add to their efficiency by mixing them together before you put them in your container.

When you create any magickal box, it's essential that you write down exactly what you want on a piece of clean white paper. For instance, if you wanted to give a wish box to a newly married couple, you'd write something like *"I desire for this union to be filled with happiness, love, and longevity. So mote it be."* Fold the paper in half, and then in half again, and place it inside the box or pouch.

It doesn't matter whether you leave your herbs in their original form as sprigs or whether you chop them. Just place your selection of herbs inside the box along with the folded paper and close the lid. If you are using a pouch, tie it up securely by either binding the top with a ribbon or pulling the drawstring tight. Once your box or pouch is filled and sealed, it is important that you charge its contents. On a clear night (making sure to avoid the dark of the moon), leave the box or sachet outside to soak up the moon's rays. The next morning, bring it inside and place it on your altar. Light a white candle and say this invocation nine times:

My magickal package is charged by the moon,

The wishes will be granted soon.

Leave the candle to burn for an hour (supervised) before blowing it out. Then put your box in a safe place, or hang your pouch or carry it around with you. Once your wish has been granted, there is no need to discard your box or pouch. You can use it again in the future.

ANGELICA ROOT: Wonderful for summoning angels and asking for protection. Hang a pouch of this in the kitchen to bless your home.

BASIL: If you are trying to get pregnant, hang a bunch of this above the bed and make love under it every night for two weeks. Basil is also commonly used in conjunction with money rituals to help boost income.

BAY: Take a handful of bay leaves and place them inside a wish box to remove curses. You can also sleep with a bay pouch under your pillow to facilitate lucid dreaming.

CATNIP: Carry catnip in your purse to attract love and popularity or to be safe when you are traveling. Witches often give catnip to their friends as a way of sealing the friendship and making sure it is long-lasting. (See "Poppy Seeds" for another way to use catnip.)

CHAMOMILE: If you or a loved one suffers from bad dreams or insomnia, or to help children sleep through the night, sprinkle a small amount of chamomile over the bedroom floor. This will induce sleep and ensure those dreams are sweet.

CHIVES: Tie a bunch of chives high above the front door to keep out unwanted spirits, or chop some finely with a knife and place them in a pouch to banish someone who is negative or harmful from your life.

CINNAMON BARK OR POWDER: A very powerful herb, cinnamon is fantastic for increasing your psychic ability or helping with healing spells. To attract wealth, carry one stick or a tiny pouch of powder in your wallet.

CLOVES: If you are grieving, cloves will bring comfort to you. For help attracting Mr. or Ms. Right, push twenty cloves into a whole orange and pop it inside a wish box.

COMFREY LEAF: Chop up fresh comfrey leaves for protection during travel; it may help the purse strings too. Good to use in a spell for settling down emotions after times of stress or for securing a new job.

DANDELION LEAF OR ROOT: Dandelion has so many uses, it's impossible to list them all. For health and well-being, separate the petals from a few flowers and carry them on your person for a week. To summon the spirits and help with divination, take the root and place it in your wish box.

DILL: When a baby is born, fill a pouch with freshly chopped dill and hang it above the nursery door. This will ensure that the child is protected and that he or she will grow up to succeed academically. Mix with lavender and elderflowers to attract romance.

ECHINACEA: Brilliant for keeping away colds and flu, so use in all healing spells for a little extra zing. Echinacea flowers can be used in a pouch to enhance meditation or scattered on the altar for money rituals.

ELDERBERRIES AND ELDERFLOWERS: Fill a pretty pouch with dried elderflower and give it to a bride on her wedding day to maket sure she remains protected and happy in her marriage. Elder is great for any romantic purpose and works beautifully if used along with rose petals.

EUCALYPTUS LEAF: If the house has a heavy feel about it or the kids are constantly bickering, use eucalyptus leaves to calm down the disruptive energies. It's also excellent when used alongside sage to ward off illness.

FEVERFEW: This herb is renowned for getting rid of headaches, but it is also beneficial for clearing your head if you have decisions to make. The best magickal feverfew is grown outside, but be warned: plant it in a pot, for it can spread rapidly if left unrestrained in your garden.

GARLIC: I doubt you will be associating with vampires, but should you happen to come across one on your travels, garlic works as a great source of protection. Hang the bulbs in doorways to ward off evil or put garlic salt in pouches and sachets to keep away any bad vibrations.

HEATHER: Heather is a very lucky herb to have in the home, and when it is hung in a window it is said to bring good fortune to the people who live there. If you feel unsafe, or if you want to try something risky like bungee jumping or skydiving, carry a few sprigs on you and you'll automatically have protection.

LAVENDER: Lavender is incorporated a lot in spell casting and has many uses; the main one is to bring a sense of calm to situations and to promote peaceful sleep. To attract a partner, carry some lavender and a piece of amethyst crystal together. They complement each other and enhance any love spell.

MANDRAKE ROOT: The mandrake root has been considered a powerful talisman since biblical times. It has long been used in witchcraft to guard against any kind of misfortune. If you have had a run of bad luck, hang a pouch of mandrake in the living area of your home and it will absorb the negativity, leaving everything neutral again. If placed on your altar, the root will enhance your magickal workings and give your spells more power.

MINT: Angels and spirits are thought to love the smell of mint, so to encourage them into your life, grow mint in the garden and cut a few bunches every now and then to bring into the house.

MISTLETOE: Just because it's hung above doorways at Christmas doesn't mean you actually want to kiss everyone who stands under it. Traditionally mistletoe was used for encouraging love and fertility, but it has other qualities too. To distance yourself from annoying people, separate the berries from the stem and dry them before placing them in a wish box or sachet. Also works in warding off illness.

MUGWORT: Mugwort can be used in nearly every spell because it boosts the spell's performance and adds a bit of extra clout. Best used for scrying, divination, and prophetic dreams.

NETTLE: If your house is haunted, nettles will drive out unwanted spirits or deflect any curses. Carefully mix nettle with mandrake to make it more powerful—but wear gloves, because nettles do sting when they come in contact with the skin.

OAK BARK: Everyone has those times in life when they need a bit of extra physical or emotional strength. Use a small piece of bark in a pouch or a box to raise your energy level and put a spring back in your step.

POPPY SEEDS: These are great for love and fertility spells and perfect for pouches. During a full moon phase, take about a teaspoon of packaged poppy seeds and put them in a sachet with a teaspoon of catnip.

ROSEMARY: Probably one of the most widely used herbs in Wicca, rosemary is good for the soul and is treated as a powerful cleanser. Use it for house blessings or mix it with mint to prepare a magickal space for a spell.

SAGE: This herb promotes wisdom and knowledge, so it is helpful to use when you have an examination or a driving test coming up. Native Americans use smudge sticks made from white sage to purify their environments, and witches have adopted this method for clearing away bad vibes. White or common sage can be used.

SAINT-JOHN'S-WORT: Magickally speaking, this herb is a wonderful protection against fire. Banish ghosts and demons by hanging a pouch of Saint-John's-wort in a high spot in the house. It also promotes psychic vision and helps you foretell the future.

VALERIAN: Fresh valerian is not easy to get hold of, but you can buy it online. In some countries, valerian is available only in powdered root form, sold in capsules in health food stores; you can use this as an alternative if the leaves are hard to come by. Placed in a wish box, valerian can ease tension and arguments. Animal spells benefit from valerian too, so if you have a problem with a pet, put some valerian on your altar.

VERVAIN: Get your wallet bursting with cash by carrying vervain in a sachet. It is also good for building up a business or seeking a promotion or a new job.

MOON PHASES AND MAGICK

Following is a list of numerous spells that you can perform during different phases of the moon—certain spells work better during particular phases. All the spells listed can be cast in a simple ritual: Take a small white candle to the window and gaze at the moon through the windowpane. Say your wish out loud and with feeling, then leave the candle to burn down and blow out (while you are still in the room, of course; do not leave the candle unattended or place it near a curtain).

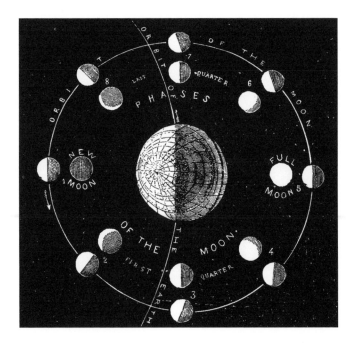

FULL MOON

From a magickal point of view the full moon does not have any
negative connotations; it is just considered a very powerful time
of the month. For some reason, Fridays that fall on full moons are
wonderful days for casting love spells. If you try casting love spells
during any other moon phase, it doesn't mean that they will not
work, but the results could take much longer. There are lots of other
spells that benefit from being cast on a full moon too, and these are
listed below:

* Protecting property and home
* Adding vigor to your life
* Anything to do with love
* Increasing self-confidence
* Advancing in career and work
* Enhancing psychic ability/clairvoyance
* Strengthening friendships and family bonds
* Performing general good-luck spells

THE WAXING MOON

When the moon is waxing, witches like to cast spells for improving
situations or for getting things going if things have been in a rut for
a while. Often, when life is unchanging, it takes a little boost to amp
things up a bit, and this phase is definitely the best time to kick-start
your life. The following spells act faster during a waxing moon:

* Moving forward from depression
* Getting out of a rut
* Passing examinations and tests

* Finding lost objects
* Healing a sick animal or finding a lost pet

THE WANING ☾☉☽

The waning moon is the perfect time to cast spells for getting rid of
the black clouds and negative energies that sometimes hang over us.
It is a time when you can draw down strength from the universe.

* Developing inner strength and assertiveness
* Banishing enemies
* Stopping arguments
* Soothing unruly children
* Calming anxiety
* Getting out of tricky situations

THE NEW ☾☉☽

The new moon phase surrounds us with lots of positive energy
and can act as a catalyst for immediate change. Many transitions
naturally happen around a new moon anyway, such as new jobs,
births, and moves, but if you need to revolutionize your life, cast
spells at this time for:

* Career changes
* Moving house swiftly and easily
* Safe and enjoyable travel
* Increasing your cash flow
* Better health
* Conceiving

THE WHEEL OF THE YEAR

Witches celebrate the eight Pagan and Celtic festivals referred to as the Wheel of the Year. This is a calendar of events beginning with Samhain, a Wiccan New Year festival, better known today as Halloween or All Hallows' Eve.

Yule–Winter Solstice

Begins December 21 ~ Ends January 1

Pronounced *Yu-la*

The time of the winter solstice when the ancient sun child is reborn again. With the love of the gods, new life is reborn, indicating a fresh start for all. Place a few sprigs of holly on the altar to represent fruitfulness and fertility.

Imbolc–Spring Begins

Begins January 31 ~ Ends sunset, February 1

Pronounced *Im-bulk*

This time marks the beginning of spring. The festival is connected with the goddess Brigid, who is said to bless the houses of people who leave her food offerings at this time. Place snowdrops on the altar to welcome in the spring.

Ostara–Spring Equinox

March 21

Pronounced *Ost-ara*

Celebrate this seasonal change as Ēostra or Ostara, the Anglo-Saxon goddess of dawn, also known as the Spring Maiden, brings new life to the soil by fertilizing the earth and nature. Place eggs on the altar to symbolize abundance and fertility.

Beltane–May Day

Begins April 30 ~ Ends May 1

Pronounced *Bell-tane*

This fire festival marks the beginning of summer and originates from the Celtic god Bel. Large fires were lit to give tribute to the sun and the ashes from the fire were believed to hold magical influence. Maypole dancing was performed to encourage Bel to bring in the light and protect the crops. Burn rose incense and sage in a cauldron on your altar to mark this occasion.

Litha–Summer Solstice

Between June 19–25

Pronounced *Lith-a*

Traditionally, many witches choose to rejoice in midsummer June 21, when we can celebrate a bountiful, first harvest with the sun (sol), the Lord of Light. He shines his light on the crops and brings warmth to the many workers who gather the yields. Pick herbs and collect magical items from the earth at this time to increase the potency of spells.

Lammas/Lughnasadh–First Harvest

Begins August 1

Pronounced *Lam-ass or Loo-nassa*

This historic Gaelic festival is recognized by the first harvest of fruits and is a time for handfastings, weddings, fetes, and contests. The grain harvest took place on this date, giving new meaning to the original term *Lammas* (Anglo-Saxon for "loaf-mass"), and great thanks was given to the goddess, the Queen of the Land. Place wheat and grain on your altar to ensure an abundance of food for the impending winter.

Mabon–Autumn Equinox

Begins September 21 ~ Ends September 24

Pronounced *May-bon*

As the warm sun begins to set, the time between day and night is equal and so the ancients sent gratitude to the gods before venturing out to harvest crops. Place foodstuffs on your altar to give thanks.

Samhain–New Year/All Hallows Eve'/Halloween

Begins October 31 ~ Ends November 1

Pronounced *Sow-en or Sow-in*

This holiday of Celtic pagan origins marks the end of summer and the onset of winter. It is an important time in the calendar to honor and give respect to the dead. A veil that separates the spirit world from the earth plane is lifted, making communications easier. Place candles and incense on the altar to connect with your loved ones in spirit.

THE BOOK
OF
SHADOWS

DATE

_____

MOON PHASE

_____

SPELL

_____

_____

_____

DATE

_____

MOON PHASE

_____

SPELL

_____

_____

_____

DATE

MOON PHASE

SPELL

DATE

_____

MOON PHASE

_____

SPELL

_____

_____

_____

DATE

_____

MOON PHASE

_____

SPELL

_____

_____

_____

DATE

_____

MOON PHASE

_____

SPELL

_____

_____

_____

DATE

_____

MOON PHASE

_____

SPELL

_____

_____

_____

DATE

MOON PHASE

SPELL

DATE

_____

MOON PHASE

_____

SPELL

_____

_____

_____

DATE

_____

MOON PHASE

_____

SPELL

_____

_____

_____

DATE

_____

MOON PHASE

_____

SPELL

_____

_____

_____

DATE

_____

MOON PHASE

_____

SPELL

_____

_____

_____

DATE

_____

MOON PHASE

_____

SPELL

_____

_____

_____

DATE

_____

MOON PHASE

_____

SPELL

_____

_____

_____

DATE

MOON PHASE

SPELL

_____

_____

_____

DATE

_____

MOON PHASE

_____

SPELL

_____

_____

_____

DATE

_____

MOON PHASE

_____

SPELL

_____

_____

_____

DATE

_____

MOON PHASE

_____

SPELL

_____

_____

_____

DATE

_____

MOON PHASE

_____

SPELL

_____

_____

_____

DATE

_____

MOON PHASE

_____

SPELL

_____

_____

_____

DATE

_____

MOON PHASE

_____

SPELL

_____

_____

_____

DATE

_____

MOON PHASE

_____

SPELL

_____

_____

_____

DATE

_____

MOON PHASE

_____

SPELL

_____

_____

_____

DATE

_____

MOON PHASE

_____

SPELL

_____

_____

_____

DATE

_____

MOON PHASE

_____

SPELL

_____

_____

_____

DATE

_____

MOON PHASE

_____

SPELL

_____

_____

_____

DATE

_____

MOON PHASE

_____

SPELL

_____

_____

_____

DATE

_____

MOON PHASE

_____

SPELL

_____

_____

_____

DATE

_____

MOON PHASE

_____

SPELL

_____

_____

_____

DATE

MOON PHASE

SPELL

_____

_____

_____

DATE

_____

MOON PHASE

_____

SPELL

_____

_____

_____

DATE

_____

MOON PHASE

_____

SPELL

_____

_____

_____

DATE

MOON PHASE

SPELL

DATE

MOON PHASE

SPELL

_____

_____

_____

DATE

MOON PHASE

SPELL

DATE

_____

MOON PHASE

_____

SPELL

_____

_____

_____

DATE

_____

MOON PHASE

_____

SPELL

_____

_____

_____

DATE

_____

MOON PHASE

_____

SPELL

_____

_____

_____

DATE

_____

MOON PHASE

_____

SPELL

_____

_____

_____

DATE

_____

MOON PHASE

_____

SPELL

_____

_____

_____

DATE

_____

MOON PHASE

_____

SPELL

_____

_____

_____

DATE

_____

MOON PHASE

_____

SPELL

_____

_____

_____

DATE
_____

MOON PHASE
_____

SPELL

_____

_____

_____

DATE

_____

MOON PHASE

_____

SPELL

_____

_____

_____

DATE

_____

MOON PHASE

_____

SPELL

_____

_____

_____

DATE

_____

MOON PHASE

_____

SPELL

_____

_____

_____

DATE

_____

MOON PHASE

_____

SPELL

_____

_____

_____

DATE

_____

MOON PHASE

_____

SPELL

_____

_____

_____

DATE

MOON PHASE

SPELL

_____

_____

_____

DATE

_____

MOON PHASE

_____

SPELL

_____

_____

_____

DATE

_____

MOON PHASE

_____

SPELL

_____

_____

_____

DATE

MOON PHASE

SPELL

DATE

_____

MOON PHASE

_____

SPELL

_____

_____

_____

DATE

_____

MOON PHASE

_____

SPELL

_____

_____

_____

DATE

_____

MOON PHASE

_____

SPELL

_____

_____

_____

DATE

_____

MOON PHASE

_____

SPELL

_____

_____

_____

DATE

_____

MOON PHASE

_____

SPELL

_____

_____

_____

DATE

_____

MOON PHASE

_____

SPELL

_____

_____

_____

DATE

_____

MOON PHASE

_____

SPELL

_____

_____

_____

DATE

_____

MOON PHASE

_____

SPELL

_____

_____

_____

DATE

_____

MOON PHASE

_____

SPELL

_____

_____

_____

DATE

_____

MOON PHASE

_____

SPELL

_____

_____

_____

DATE

_____

MOON PHASE

_____

SPELL

_____

_____

_____

DATE

_____

MOON PHASE

_____

SPELL

_____

_____

_____

DATE

_____

MOON PHASE

_____

SPELL

_____

_____

_____

DATE

_____

MOON PHASE

_____

SPELL

_____

_____

_____

DATE

_____

MOON PHASE

_____

SPELL

_____

_____

_____

DATE

_____

MOON PHASE

_____

SPELL

_____

_____

_____

DATE

_____

MOON PHASE

_____

SPELL

_____

_____

_____

DATE

_____

MOON PHASE

_____

SPELL

_____

_____

_____

DATE

_____

MOON PHASE

_____

SPELL

_____

_____

_____

DATE

MOON PHASE

SPELL

_____

_____

_____

DATE

_____

MOON PHASE

_____

SPELL

_____

_____

_____

DATE

_____

MOON PHASE

_____

SPELL

_____

_____

_____

DATE

_____

MOON PHASE

_____

SPELL

_____

_____

_____

DATE

_____

MOON PHASE

_____

SPELL

_____

_____

_____

DATE

_____

MOON PHASE

_____

SPELL

_____

_____

_____

DATE

_____

MOON PHASE

_____

SPELL

_____

_____

_____

DATE

_____

MOON PHASE

_____

SPELL

_____

_____

_____

DATE

_____

MOON PHASE

_____

SPELL

_____

_____

_____

DATE

_____

MOON PHASE

_____

SPELL

_____

_____

_____

DATE

_____

MOON PHASE

_____

SPELL

_____

_____

_____

DATE

_____

MOON PHASE

_____

SPELL

_____

_____

_____

DATE

_____

MOON PHASE

_____

SPELL

_____

_____

_____

DATE

_____

MOON PHASE

_____

SPELL

_____

_____

_____

_____

DATE

MOON PHASE

SPELL

_____

_____

_____

DATE

_____

MOON PHASE

_____

SPELL

_____

_____

_____

DATE

MOON PHASE

SPELL

DATE

_____

MOON PHASE

_____

SPELL

_____

_____

_____

DATE

MOON PHASE

SPELL

_____

_____

_____

DATE

_____

MOON PHASE

_____

SPELL

_____

_____

_____

DATE

_____

MOON PHASE

_____

SPELL

_____

_____

_____

DATE

_____

MOON PHASE

_____

SPELL

_____

_____

_____

DATE

MOON PHASE

SPELL

_____

_____

_____

DATE

_____

MOON PHASE

_____

SPELL

_____

_____

_____

DATE

_____

MOON PHASE

_____

SPELL

_____

_____

_____

DATE

_____

MOON PHASE

_____

SPELL

_____

_____

_____

DATE

MOON PHASE

SPELL

DATE

_____

MOON PHASE

_____

SPELL

_____

_____

_____

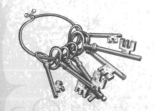

DATE

_____

MOON PHASE

_____

SPELL

_____

_____

_____

DATE

_____

MOON PHASE

_____

SPELL

_____

_____

_____

DATE

MOON PHASE

SPELL

DATE

_____

MOON PHASE

_____

SPELL

_____

_____

_____

DATE

MOON PHASE

SPELL

_____

_____

_____

DATE

_____

MOON PHASE

_____

SPELL

_____

_____

_____

DATE

MOON PHASE

SPELL

DATE

_____

MOON PHASE

_____

SPELL

_____

_____

_____

DATE

_____

MOON PHASE

_____

SPELL

_____

_____

_____

DATE

_____

MOON PHASE

_____

SPELL

_____

_____

_____

_____

DATE

MOON PHASE

SPELL

DATE

_____

MOON PHASE

_____

SPELL

_____

_____

_____

DATE

_____

MOON PHASE

_____

SPELL

_____

_____

_____

DATE
_____

MOON PHASE
_____

SPELL

_____
_____
_____

DATE

MOON PHASE

SPELL

DATE

_____

MOON PHASE

_____

SPELL

_____

_____

_____

DATE

_____

MOON PHASE

_____

SPELL

_____

_____

_____

DATE

_____

MOON PHASE

_____

SPELL

_____

_____

_____

DATE

MOON PHASE

SPELL

DATE

_____

MOON PHASE

_____

SPELL

_____

_____

_____

DATE

_____

MOON PHASE

_____

SPELL

_____

_____

_____

DATE

_____

MOON PHASE

_____

SPELL

_____

_____

_____

DATE

MOON PHASE

SPELL

DATE

MOON PHASE

SPELL

DATE

_____

MOON PHASE

_____

SPELL

_____

_____

_____

DATE

_____

MOON PHASE

_____

SPELL

_____

_____

_____

DATE

MOON PHASE

SPELL

_____

_____

_____

DATE

_____

MOON PHASE

_____

SPELL

_____

_____

_____

DATE

_____

MOON PHASE

_____

SPELL

.

_____

_____

_____

DATE

_____

MOON PHASE

_____

SPELL

_____

_____

_____

DATE

_____

MOON PHASE

_____

SPELL

_____

_____

_____

DATE

MOON PHASE

SPELL

_____

_____

_____

DATE

MOON PHASE

SPELL

DATE

MOON PHASE

SPELL

DATE

MOON PHASE

SPELL

_____

_____

_____

DATE

_____

MOON PHASE

_____

SPELL

_____

_____

_____

DATE

_____

MOON PHASE

_____

SPELL

_____

_____

_____

DATE

_____

MOON PHASE

_____

SPELL

_____

_____

_____

DATE

_____

MOON PHASE

_____

SPELL

_____

_____

_____

DATE

MOON PHASE

SPELL

DATE

MOON PHASE

SPELL

DATE

_____

MOON PHASE

_____

SPELL

_____

_____

_____

DATE

_____

MOON PHASE

_____

SPELL

_____

_____

_____

DATE

_____

MOON PHASE

_____

SPELL

_____

_____

_____

DATE

_____

MOON PHASE

_____

SPELL

_____

_____

_____

DATE

_____

MOON PHASE

_____

SPELL

_____

_____

_____

DATE

_____

MOON PHASE

_____

SPELL

_____

_____

_____

DATE

MOON PHASE

SPELL

_____

_____

_____

DATE

_____

MOON PHASE

_____

SPELL

_____

_____

_____

DATE

_____

MOON PHASE

_____

SPELL

_____

_____

_____

DATE

_____

MOON PHASE

_____

SPELL

_____

_____

_____

DATE

MOON PHASE

SPELL

DATE

MOON PHASE

SPELL

DATE

_____

MOON PHASE

_____

SPELL

_____

_____

_____

_____

DATE

_____

MOON PHASE

_____

SPELL

_____

_____

_____

DATE

_____

MOON PHASE

_____

SPELL

_____

_____

_____

DATE

_____

MOON PHASE

_____

SPELL

_____

_____

_____

DATE

MOON PHASE

SPELL

_____

_____

_____

DATE

_____

MOON PHASE

_____

SPELL

_____

_____

_____

DATE

_____

MOON PHASE

_____

SPELL

_____

_____

_____

DATE

MOON PHASE

SPELL

_____

_____

_____

DATE

_____

MOON PHASE

_____

SPELL

_____

_____

_____

DATE

_____

MOON PHASE

_____

SPELL

_____

_____

_____

DATE

_____

MOON PHASE

_____

SPELL

_____

_____

_____

DATE

_____

MOON PHASE

_____

SPELL

_____

_____

_____

DATE

_____

MOON PHASE

_____

SPELL

_____

_____

_____

DATE

_____

MOON PHASE

_____

SPELL

_____

_____

_____

DATE

_____

MOON PHASE

_____

SPELL

_____

_____

_____

DATE

MOON PHASE

SPELL

_____

_____

_____

DATE

MOON PHASE

SPELL

DATE

_____

MOON PHASE

_____

SPELL

_____

_____

_____

DATE

_____

MOON PHASE

_____

SPELL

_____

_____

_____

DATE

_____

MOON PHASE

_____

SPELL

_____

_____

_____

DATE

_____

MOON PHASE

_____

SPELL

_____

_____

_____

DATE

_____

MOON PHASE

_____

SPELL

_____

_____

_____

DATE

_____

MOON PHASE

_____

SPELL

_____

_____

_____

DATE

_____

MOON PHASE

_____

SPELL

_____

_____

_____

DATE

_____

MOON PHASE

_____

SPELL

_____

_____

_____

DATE

_____

MOON PHASE

_____

SPELL

_____

_____

_____

DATE

_____

MOON PHASE

_____

SPELL

_____

_____

_____

DATE

_____

MOON PHASE

_____

SPELL

_____

_____

_____

DATE

_____

MOON PHASE

_____

SPELL

_____

_____

_____

DATE

_____

MOON PHASE

_____

SPELL

_____

_____

_____

DATE

_____

MOON PHASE

_____

SPELL

_____

_____

_____

DATE

_____

MOON PHASE

_____

SPELL

_____

_____

_____

DATE

_____

MOON PHASE

_____

SPELL

_____

_____

_____

DATE

_____

MOON PHASE

_____

SPELL

_____

_____

_____

DATE

_____

MOON PHASE

_____

SPELL

_____

_____

_____

DATE

MOON PHASE

SPELL

DATE

MOON PHASE

SPELL

DATE

_____

MOON PHASE

_____

SPELL

_____

_____

_____

DATE

MOON PHASE

SPELL

SPELL

_____

_____

_____

DATE

MOON PHASE

SPELL

_____
_____
_____

DATE

MOON PHASE

SPELL

DATE

_____

MOON PHASE

_____

SPELL

_____

_____

_____

DATE

_____

MOON PHASE

_____

SPELL

_____

_____

_____

DATE

MOON PHASE

SPELL

_____
_____
_____

DATE

_____

MOON PHASE

_____

SPELL

_____

_____

_____

DATE

_____

MOON PHASE

_____

SPELL

_____

_____

_____

DATE

_____

MOON PHASE

_____

SPELL

_____

_____

_____

DATE

_____

MOON PHASE

_____

SPELL

_____

_____

_____

DATE

_____

MOON PHASE

_____

SPELL

_____

_____

_____

DATE

_____

MOON PHASE

_____

SPELL

_____

_____

_____

DATE

_____

MOON PHASE

_____

SPELL

_____

_____

_____

DATE

_____

MOON PHASE

_____

SPELL

_____

_____

_____

DATE

_____

MOON PHASE

_____

SPELL

_____

_____

_____

DATE

_____

MOON PHASE

_____

SPELL

_____

_____

_____

DATE

_____

MOON PHASE

_____

SPELL

_____

_____

_____

DATE

_____

MOON PHASE

_____

SPELL

_____

_____

_____

DATE

_____

MOON PHASE

_____

SPELL

_____

_____

_____

DATE

_____

MOON PHASE

_____

SPELL

_____

_____

_____

_____

DATE

MOON PHASE

SPELL

DATE

_____

MOON PHASE

_____

SPELL

_____

_____

_____

DATE

MOON PHASE

SPELL

DATE

_____

MOON PHASE

_____

SPELL

_____

_____

_____

DATE

_____

MOON PHASE

_____

SPELL

_____

_____

_____

DATE

_____

MOON PHASE

_____

SPELL

_____

_____

_____

DATE

_____

MOON PHASE

_____

SPELL

_____

_____

_____

DATE

MOON PHASE

SPELL

_____

_____

_____

DATE

_____

MOON PHASE

_____

SPELL

_____

_____

_____

DATE

_____

MOON PHASE

_____

SPELL

_____

_____

_____

DATE

MOON PHASE

SPELL

DATE

_____

MOON PHASE

_____

SPELL

_____

_____

_____